Home Invasion

Monique Polak

orca soundings

ORCA BOOK PUBLISHERS

Copyright © Monique Polak 2005

Library and Archives Canada Cataloguing in Publication

Polak, Monique
Home invasion / Monique Polak.

(Orca soundings)
ISBN 1-55143-482-2

I. Title. II. Series.

PS8631.O43H64 2005   jC813'.6   C2005-904465-9

First published in the United States, 2005
Library of Congress Control Number: 2005930532

Summary: While a home invader terrorizes the city,
Josh finds himself sneaking into other people's houses.

Orca Book Publishers gratefully acknowledges the support for its publishing
programs provided by the following agencies: the Government of Canada
through the Book Publishing Industry Development Program and the
Canada Council for the Arts, and the Province of British Columbia through
the BC Arts Council and the Book Publishing Tax Credit.

Cover design: Lynn O'Rourke
Cover photography: Getty Images

Orca Book Publishers
PO Box 5626, Stn. B
Victoria, BC Canada
V8R 6S4

Orca Book Publishers
PO Box 468
Custer, WA USA
98240-0468

www.orcabook.com
Printed and bound in Canada.
010 09 08 07 • 5 4 3 2

For Mike and Ali, with love

Acknowledgments

Thanks to Viva Singer, Claire Holden Rothman, Evadne Anderson and my mother, Celine Polak, for reading this manuscript in its earliest stages; to my students Lee Rovinescu and Anthony Bossy for the basketball lessons; to Rina Singh and Elaine Kalman Naves for their continuing encouragement; to Barbara Vininsky and my friends at the Jack and Jill Shop; to my editor, Andrew Wooldridge, for his good sense and sharp eye, and to the rest of the team at Orca. Finally, thanks to my daughter, Alicia Melamed, and my husband, Michael Shenker. Their humor and love make all things possible.

Chapter One

Don't ask me what she sees in him. He's not handsome, that's for sure. He's got chipmunk cheeks and this weird cowlick that looks like a rhino's horn. She thinks he's funny, but then Mom's always had a bizarre sense of humor.

The two of them were at it again last night.

My room's right next to theirs, and the walls are paper-thin. I could hear their bed creaking. I tried pulling the pillow over my head, but then I heard Mom's voice, soft and low.

She kept whispering the same disgusting thing—over and over again.

"Shh, Clay," she kept saying. "We don't want to wake Josh up."

As if I wasn't already awake.

How do they expect me to look at them in the morning?

I was sitting in the kitchen reading the comics. Mom was just leaving for a run. The last thing she said to me was "Don't let the home invader in!"

Everyone in Montreal's talking about the home invader. He's some guy—or maybe it's a girl (I don't want to be sexist here)—who robs houses while the people who live in them are home. You gotta admit, it's pretty creepy. Bad enough getting burgled when you're out, but imagine it happening when you're right there.

Mom was already out the door, so she didn't hear what I muttered under my breath: "You already let him in."

Of course I was talking about Clay. Her new husband. My stepfather. Montreal's number one home invader.

Things were going fine before Clay moved in. Him and all his stuff. His maroon bathrobe, his weird recipes, his old turntable—who listens to vinyl anymore?—and the little scraps of paper he's always doodling on.

As I was thinking that, Clay rushed downstairs. The guy's always in a hurry, late for one thing or another. He had a big white blob of shaving cream smack in the middle of his chin. If I were nicer, I'd tell him.

But I'm not that nice.

"Have you seen my keys, kiddo?" he asked.

I shrugged. If he were normal, he'd use the key holder that's hanging in the front hallway. It's got little hooks, and it's shaped like a key, so you'd think he'd figure out what it's meant for. But Clay is not exactly normal. He rifled through a pile of papers on the desk in the corridor, adding to the mess. I wondered if he thought about checking his pockets.

I heard him opening the front closet. From where I was sitting in the kitchen, I could only see the soles of his feet. He was on his knees, taking stuff out. I spotted a pair of skates and the box where we kept mittens. Didn't he realize it was July? Why would his keys be in with the winter stuff?

Suddenly he started talking to himself. "We need to do something about this closet," he said. Then he started emptying the whole thing out. I could hear him dragging out the vacuum cleaner and some suitcases. I bet he had forgotten about the keys altogether. Which would be just like Clay. He's not exactly focused. Mom says it's because he has an artistic personality—and that that's one of the things she loves about him—but if you ask me, that's just an excuse. In my opinion, the guy's a disaster.

He had emptied so much crap into the corridor, I could barely see the front door. Then he stood up again, surveying his work.

"There you are, you little bugger," I heard him say. Then his voice dropped. "Right in my front pocket." I tried not to laugh.

Now that he had found his keys, he would probably forget about putting the stuff back in the closet. If I did that, Mom would have a fit. But she never, ever gets mad at Clay. It's one more thing I hate about him.

The doorbell rang. I could hear Clay wade through the mess he had made.

I put the comics down and headed out into the corridor. It looked like a war zone. A girl and a middle-aged woman were standing in our vestibule. They didn't look like home invaders. Besides, home invaders don't use the bell.

"I'm Annette Levesque," the woman said, reaching out to shake Clay's hand. She looked tired. "This is my daughter, Patsy." Patsy smiled. She had braces and wavy brown hair. You could tell she'd rather not be here. "We just moved in two doors down and we're wondering if you have an X-Acto knife we could borrow. Ours is in a box somewhere."

"We need an X-Acto knife so we can open boxes and find our X-Acto knife," Patsy explained.

I laughed. "I'll get it. By the way," I said before I headed back to the kitchen for the knife, "I'm Josh." I lifted my chin toward my stepfather. "He's Clay."

"Welcome to the 'hood," Clay said.

Why did he have to say 'hood? He's such a loser.

When I got back with the knife, Clay and Mrs. Levesque were discussing recipes. "I wish Sylvain would help with the cooking. Maybe you'll be a good influence," she said.

Good influence? She's got to be kidding! Last night Clay invented a new recipe—pasta with peanut butter. I wondered what Patsy would think of that.

As I handed Patsy the knife the phone rang. Clay picked it up. I could tell from the way Mrs. Levesque and Patsy were shuffling that they wanted to leave, but they thought it'd be bad manners not to say good-bye first. Now they were stuck waiting for Clay to get off the phone.

"Are you going to Royal Crest in the fall?" I asked Patsy.

"Uh-huh," she said, "grade ten. How about you?"

"Me too." I wanted to tell her I could introduce her to some people, but I was listening in on the phone call.

Clay raised his voice, which meant he was probably talking to my gramma in Toronto, who's hard of hearing. "What's the phone number there, Tammy? Of course, if you need her, she'll come. No, no, she'll want to be there with you. She's out for a run, but I'll have her phone you the minute she gets in." He checked his watch.

I was right. It was my grandmother. Something must be wrong.

"Is Gramps all right?" I asked Clay.

He didn't answer. He wrote the number on a slip of paper.

"We really should be going," Mrs. Levesque whispered.

When I followed her and Patsy to the door, Mrs. Levesque squinted at me, like she was studying my face. "You have your dad's eyes," she said.

One of Clay's flip-flops was lying on the

floor in the hallway. I gave it a kick so that, for a second, it flew up into the air. "He's not my dad," I told her.

Chapter Two

"At least this'll give you two an opportunity to bond," Mom told us when we dropped her off at the airport.

Gramps had a heart attack. The good news was he was going to be okay; there wasn't much damage to his heart. The bad news was Gramma had flipped out, and needed Mom to be with her in Toronto for at least a week. Which meant I was stuck with Clay.

I felt like puking when they gave each other one of those big mushy kisses. Instead I turned away and counted to five, hoping that when I was done the two lovebirds would be through. It was a good thing she had a plane to catch or they might still be at it.

On the way home, I made a point of not saying a word to Clay. I could tell from the way he tapped the steering wheel that I was making him uncomfortable. That cheered me up a little.

There was a slimy brown apple core at the edge of the floor mat, near my right foot.

"Oops," Clay said when he noticed me looking down at it. "I didn't want to throw it out the window."

"Do you have a bag in here for garbage?" I asked him.

He pointed to the glove compartment, but when I opened it, all this junk came tumbling out onto my lap. Crumpled-up maps, candy wrappers, parking tickets and car wash coupons. I couldn't help laughing.

"What's so funny?" Clay asked. "I told you there was a bag in there," he added triumphantly, pointing to a tattered plastic bag balled up in the back corner of the glove compartment.

"What do you feel like having for supper?" he asked me when we're turning the corner and heading onto our block.

I knew what I didn't feel like having. Pasta with peanut butter. "Whatever," I told him, shrugging my shoulders.

"Well then, I guess I'll invent something."

My heart sank. What was he going to do—add jam to the recipe?

"I'm going to shoot some hoops," I told him as we pulled into the driveway. I hoped that maybe I'd bump into Patsy, the girl from that morning, on the way to the park

I was dribbling my basketball down the sidewalk when I noticed a telephone company van parked outside Patsy's house. They were probably getting their phone hooked up.

When I got closer, I noticed the garage door was half open. I slowed down for a better look. Maybe Patsy's dad was doing some yard work. But there was no sign of anyone.

I looked over my shoulder. Nobody was watching. Then, just like that, I walked into the garage. It was like I was on autopilot. I didn't know what made me do it. Curiosity, I guess.

I remembered something we learned in English. This guy, Edgar Allan Poe, came up with an idea he called "the imp of the perverse." Mr. Johnston—I had him for English last year—said it's like when you see a sign that says *Wet paint. Don't touch*, and you have this overwhelming urge to touch it. It was like that with the Levesques' garage door. If it hadn't been open, I never would've thought of going inside.

My heart was thumping like crazy, and I was sweating. The weirdest part was I didn't think I ever felt more alive. Or more excited.

The garage was filled with cardboard boxes, stacked one on top of the other. They were all labeled. *Kitchen—pots. Dining room—fragile—good china. Pats,* which I figured was short for Patsy. I spotted some barbells on the floor. They were probably her dad's.

A steel door led into the house. I turned the handle, sure it would be locked. But it wasn't. I was in the basement. There wasn't much light and the air smelled like old socks.

I heard a voice from upstairs. It was Patsy, saying something about a phone jack.

"Annette, do you really think it's a good idea to let Pats have a phone in her room?" a man's voice asked.

"I promised her she could," Patsy's mother said.

"Next thing she'll be wanting her own number."

"Now that you mention it, Dad..." Patsy's laugh sounded like bells.

Careful not to make any noise, I sat down on the wooden steps that led from the basement up to the next floor. Now they were all laughing. Patsy, her mom and dad, and someone else. Did Patsy have a brother—or was the guy from the phone company in on the joke?

My heart was still thumping. What would I say if they found me? That I was on my way to the park when I decided to drop by? I knew I should leave, but it was like some gravitational force was keeping me there. Besides, it felt good to hear them laughing.

"Okay, that's a long-enough coffee-break!" Mrs. Levesque was saying, and I heard a box being lugged across the floor. "Let's get a few more boxes unpacked, shall we?"

Someone tore open a box.

"What did you think of Josh?" Mrs. Levesque asked. Even though the basement was cool, I felt my face turn hot. It isn't too often you get a chance to hear what people have to say about you when you're not there. Or when they don't know you are.

"He's okay," Patsy said. I couldn't help feeling disappointed. Then Patsy said something else. It was either "He's not my type" or "He is my type." The sound was muffled, so I couldn't tell for sure.

"Clay seems pleasant," Mrs. Levesque observed. "I gather he's the stepfather."

"Too bad about the corny sense of humor," Patsy said. She might not have the best taste in guys, but the girl wasn't stupid.

I couldn't make out what Mrs. Levesque said next because the phone guy interrupted. "The jacks are installed," he said.

He must have been wearing work boots because I could hear heavy footsteps on the floor above me. The sound came closer.

I couldn't keep sitting on the stairs. I headed for the nearest hiding place—the crawl space underneath the stairway. The air smelled even mustier here, and there were hard black pellets on the ground that felt rough against my knees. Mouse droppings, maybe. It was so dark that I didn't notice an old steamer trunk until I bumped into it.

"Did you hear something?" Mrs. Levesque asked. When she opened the basement door, a ray of light shone in like a spotlight. I took a deep breath.

"It's these old houses," the phone guy said. "Everything creaks."

I almost sighed with relief, but, of course, I couldn't. I didn't even breathe as he walked down the stairs. He was so close I could see that the soles of his boots were worn.

My heart thumped even faster. Sure, I was

doing something wrong, but it was definitely giving me an adrenaline rush. This must be what it feels like to be a home invader.

Chapter Three

Most people can tell when you want to be left alone. But not Clay.

The next morning I was sitting on a stool in the kitchen, trying to read the comics. I didn't mind that he was in the kitchen too, reading the front page of the paper. What I did mind was how he kept interrupting me.

"Rash of home invasions continues," he read aloud.

"Uh-huh," I said without lifting my eyes

from the comics. I was almost at my favorite, the *Wizard of Id*.

"This guy sounds like a real nut," Clay said.

"Uh-huh."

Instead of taking the hint that he was getting on my nerves, Clay started reading the whole article out loud. To make matters worse, he dropped his voice to make it sound like he was a TV announcer.

"The home invader who first struck Montreal last month is at it again." He was reading slowly. I tried sighing loudly, but he just kept reading. "Yesterday afternoon, a bungalow on the Lachine Canal was invaded. Preliminary reports suggest the culprit is the same person responsible for the six other home invasions reported in the Montreal area."

Clay paused to come up for air. Then he gave me a look, like he was expecting me to say something.

"Wow," I said in a flat voice.

Clay shook his head and continued reading. I was starting to feel like I'd never get to the *Wizard of Id*.

"Police have not released the names of the home invader's latest victims. 'Indications are that the suspect is becoming bolder,' said Marie Leduc, a police spokesperson. 'The victims of the first six home invasions were elderly, all of whom had difficulty getting around. But the latest victims are a young family. A father, mother and two children.'"

I put down the comics and looked at Clay. It sounded like the home invader was becoming more daring. This time Clay didn't notice me. At least now he was reading more quickly.

"Leduc said there are no new leads in the case. 'What makes this case particularly difficult is that the home invader is masked and has left nothing behind to aid in identifying him or her. Another factor that has been complicating our investigation is that the home invader's victims have undergone a terrible trauma. They have witnessed the invasion of their homes; they have been tied up and gagged, their possessions stolen. Despite their willingness to cooperate with us, none of the victims can recall specific details about the perpetrator of these crimes.'

"Leduc encouraged anyone with information about the home invader to contact the authorities."

"I sure hope they catch him," Clay said, folding the newspaper in half and taking a bite out of the French toast he'd made for breakfast.

"Me too," I said. I thought I had better at least pretend to eat. I cut into the French toast on my plate. I couldn't help wincing when I took a bite.

"What's in this?" I asked, reaching for a glass of water. With any luck it would help drown out the taste.

"Lemon. How'd you like it?" I could tell from the way Clay was smiling that he was really proud of his latest invention.

"I don't," I said, pushing my plate away. Even the smell was making me gag. Who would eat French toast that smelled like furniture polish?

I could tell I'd hurt his feelings. "I guess it's your artistic personality," I muttered.

That cheered him up. If there is one thing Clay likes talking about, it's art. And himself.

"You're probably right, kiddo. I like experimenting. Not just on canvas, but in the kitchen too."

"Listen," I said, clearing my throat, "could you stop calling me kiddo?"

Clay looked at me like he'd never really seen me before. "Sure, kid–" He stopped himself. Then he shrugged his shoulders. "I didn't know it bugged you."

That wasn't all that bugged me. From my seat in the kitchen, I could see right into the dining room. Or what used to be the dining room. Now it was Clay's studio. Two huge canvases were propped up against the wall. One of them was blank. The other had two bright orange blobs on it. Blobs were Clay's specialty. The amazing thing was that there were people who actually bought them. There's no accounting for taste.

"Look, Josh," Clay said more seriously. "There's something I need to talk to you about."

I hoped it didn't have to do with dinner. I'd had enough of his experiments for one day, thank you very much.

"I signed you up for basketball camp at the community center. It starts tomorrow morning at 8:15," he said.

"You what?"

"I signed you up for basketball camp," Clay repeated. Did he really think I hadn't heard him the first time?

"Didn't you think you should ask me about it first?"

Clay ran his fingers through his cowlick. He does that whenever he's nervous.

"Well, I…uh…I figured you'd be glad about it. Seeing as how you like basketball. Besides, Josh, I need quiet when I'm painting."

So that's what this was all about. His blobs.

"I'm not going to basketball camp," I told him. "You're making a unilateral decision." I knew the word "unilateral" because there's another thing Mom and Clay do in the bedroom: they discuss these stepparenting manuals Mom is always reading. According to all the manuals, stepparents should never make unilateral decisions, and they shouldn't discipline their stepchildren—at least not for the first few years.

"You're going," Clay said. "And that's that."

Truth was, I might not have minded so much—if only it wasn't Clay's idea.

Chapter Four

"Your turn, Cooper!"

The coach didn't need to call my name. The second I got my fingers on the ball, I was off, dribbling down to the other end of the gym. I might not be as tall as some of the other guys, but I'm fast—and scrappy.

We had to dribble past these orange plastic cones the coach and his assistants had set the length of the court. The idea was to get past the cones on our first try, to get past them quickly on the second, then to get past them without looking on the third, and finally, to get past them quickly, without looking. Now that was tough.

I love the sound a basketball makes when it hits the floor—or the pavement. It's a steady rhythm, kind of like a heartbeat.

"Not bad!" the coach said, slapping my arm when the drills were over.

We were practicing our jump shots when I realized I recognized the tall redheaded guy standing next to me. His jersey was soaked with sweat. "You go to Royal Crest, right?" I asked him.

"Yup," he answered. He didn't have the ball, but he was practicing just the same. He jumped in the air, then tossed an invisible ball into the net.

He turned to face me. "I'm Bobby Lambert. You're Cooper, right?"

"Josh Cooper."

"How are you liking basketball camp?" he asked me.

I couldn't help looking to see if anyone was listening. Clay was at home painting, but I definitely wouldn't have wanted him to hear what I was about to say. "It's way cool," I told Bobby.

"What're you two ladies yakking about?" the coach called out. "We're working on jump shots here!"

Bobby and I walked out of the community center together at the end of the day. It turned out he lived a couple of blocks over from our place.

It was late afternoon, but the sun was still shining brightly and the air was hot and humid.

"Ever think of trying out for the school team?" he asked me. We'd stopped to take a break on the stairs outside Ben & Jerry's on Monkland Avenue.

I told him I didn't think I was good enough to make the school team.

"You might feel different after a month at basketball camp," Bobby said.

I hoped he was right.

Bobby checked his watch. Then he reached for the sports bag he'd left on the stairs and slung it over his shoulders. "Hey, Josh," he said as he got up from the stairs, "we'd better get a move on. My folks are going out of town tomorrow. I told them I'd be around tonight. You know—family time."

I nodded. But what I was really thinking was how I didn't know the first thing about family time.

I trudged along the sidewalk, my basketball cradled in the crook of my arm. I thought about how my parents had split up so long ago I couldn't even remember when we'd been a family. Then there were all those years of just me and Mom, and spending weekends with my dad when he wasn't traveling for work. He was in China now, helping to build a new bridge. At least he'd be back in Canada for the last two weeks of July.

I swatted at a fly buzzing near my head. I thought about how I'd always missed having a real family. A mom and a dad who got along, who lived in the same house, and maybe even a big brother to show me basketball moves—or a younger one to teach them to.

"We're going to be a real family now,"
Mom told me just before Clay moved in with
us. But Mom had been wrong.

I was turning the corner to my street when I
spotted the key. Because of the way the sun
was shining, it glistened. Someone had left
it right in the lock of their front door.

The house was a small red-brick cottage
that looked a lot like ours. I walked up the
front stairs and raised my finger to the doorbell. My plan was to let whoever lived there
know they'd forgotten the key.

White lacy curtains hung in the front window. There was no one in the living room, but
I thought I heard laughter coming from the
back of the house. I didn't ring the doorbell.
I turned the doorknob and let myself in.

The air smelled of tomato sauce. The
sharp, tangy smell reminded me that all I'd
had for lunch was a ham-and-cheese sand-
wich and an apple. There was a white pillar
just past the front hallway. If I had to, I could
duck behind it. And from beside it, I'd get a
good view of whatever was going on.

A fluttering sound interrupted my thoughts. Where was it coming from?

"Boid!" a girl's voice cried out. "Come here this instant!"

The girl—she looked as if she was about seventeen—was sitting at a computer in a sunny room off the kitchen. The family room. Just thinking the words made my shoulders tense up. I watched as a small green and yellow parakeet landed on the girl's shoulder.

A younger boy—the girl's brother, probably—was sitting next to her on a colorful rug, building something out of Lego. When I craned my neck, I could see that a man was helping him.

"Hey, Dad, give me that piece!" the boy said.

The dad laughed and rumpled his son's curly hair. "Come on. We promised Mom we'd set the table," he said, using one elbow to push himself up from the rug.

I knew I should leave—I could go back outside right then and ring the bell, let them know about the key in the door—but for some reason I couldn't move from my spot.

My legs and feet felt heavy, as if I was in a dream I couldn't wake up from.

All I could see of the mom was her back. Her hair was as curly as the boy's was. "The spaghetti will be ready in five minutes!" she called, wiping her hands on her apron. "Didn't you guys promise to set the table?"

I followed her gaze as she looked toward the dining room, which opened out from the side of the kitchen. Inside was a large round table made of dark wood and surrounded by matching chairs. There were no canvases propped up against the walls like at our house, no paint-splattered sheets on the floor.

Just then, Boid, who'd been perched on the girl's shoulder, took off and flew across the room. As I ducked behind the pillar, I saw the bird make a poop that landed smack on the middle of the dining room table. I covered my mouth so I wouldn't laugh.

"Would you put that damned bird back in his cage?" the mother shouted. Her voice had turned shrill and it sounded like she was stomping her feet.

Careful not to make any noise, I tiptoed back to the front door and let myself out of the house. But before I left, I took the key from the lock and left it on the floor in the front hallway.

After all, I didn't want the home invader to get in.

Chapter Five

When I got home from camp on Wednesday, Clay was sprawled on the couch, reading some mystery.

"Aren't you supposed to be painting?" I asked as I unlaced my high-tops.

Clay looked at me over the edge of his book. He was wearing his maroon housecoat, and his reading glasses were slipping off his nose. "You can't force your muse. Sometimes taking a break can be an essential part of the artistic process."

Did he really think I cared about him and his muse? "You sent me to camp so you could paint—not lie around and read," I muttered.

Clay put his book down on the couch. "Are you saying you're not enjoying basketball camp?"

Rather than answering straightaway, I looked around. There was a huge pile of mail and flyers spilling off the little table in the front hallway. I could barely see the kitchen counter because of all the pots and pans on it. "That's right. I'm not," I said as I headed up to my bedroom.

There was junk on the stairs, too—books, the laundry basket, tubes of paint. "When's Mom coming home?" I called out.

Clay had gone back to his book. "Looks like another week," he said. "At least."

I sighed.

There was a letter from my dad on my bedroom floor. I could tell it was from him because of the handwriting and the colorful stamps. Clay must've slid it under my door. I closed the door, flopped down on my bed and tore open the envelope.

He wasn't coming in July. He was really sorry, but they were at a critical stage in the bridge project, and he couldn't get away. Maybe, he wrote, he'd be able to come in January. Or maybe I could come to China over the Christmas holidays. Didn't that sound like a great idea? He knew I'd understand, and he promised to write again soon. Love, Dad.

What a bummer, I thought. I watched my reflection in the mirror across from my bed. I had my dad's curly hair and brown eyes, but I was starting to forget what he looked like. I hadn't seen him in eleven months. That was almost a year. It wasn't right.

Wait until Mom heard. They didn't exactly get along, which might explain why they got divorced. She was always going on about how Dad didn't keep his promises or meet his obligations. Now she'd have more ammunition to use against him.

There was a knock at my door. "Everything okay in there?" Clay asked.

"Don't come in," I told him.

I waited for him to leave, but he didn't

budge. I could hear him breathing. Why didn't he just leave me alone?

"Everything okay with your dad?"

I ignored the question.

"How about a cup of tea?"

"No thanks." I tried to keep my voice calm.

I felt a little better when I heard him head downstairs. But then I heard him stop on the landing. "You sure about the tea? We've got some Chinese oolong," he called.

"I'm sure!" I didn't mean to yell. It's just how it came out.

"What time did you say your friend is coming for supper?" Clay called from the kitchen when I came downstairs about half an hour later.

"Six thirty." I'd almost forgotten Bobby was coming. He'd invited himself, really. He'd been complaining about having to eat frozen pizza pockets all week while his parents were away. "What kind of grub do you get over at your house?" he'd wanted to know. So I invited him for dinner—though I made sure to warn him about Clay's cooking.

"Do you need some help in there?" I asked Clay. I didn't really feel like helping, but I figured I should at least offer.

I could hear him chopping away. "Nah," he said, "go relax. Your friend will be here soon."

Bobby showed up early. "I was starving," he explained when I opened the door to let him in. "Hey, what's going on in here?" Bobby waved his hands in the air.

That's when I noticed the smoke. A weird thing about smoke is that sometimes, when you're in a place, you don't notice it building up. But when I turned around to lead Bobby into the kitchen, the whole first floor of the house was gray with smoke.

"Pleased to meet you, Bobby," Clay called out. All we could see of him was his maroon housecoat. The burners on the stove were glowing bright red. There were pots and pans everywhere. Not just on the stove and the counter; there was even a pot by Clay's feet.

"For potato peels," he explained when he caught me looking at it. "I hope you like

Indian food," he told Bobby. "I'm making chicken curry."

"Sounds great," Bobby said.

Suck up, I thought.

"Why don't you guys open the windows?" Clay said.

By the time the smoke cleared, dinner was ready. We sat at the kitchen table.

"Not too hot for you?" Clay asked when Bobby bit into the chicken curry.

Bobby's face was red. "It's a little spicy," he said. But that didn't stop him from asking for seconds.

I passed on the seconds.

"This yogurt sauce has a cooling effect," Clay said, passing it to Bobby.

"I don't need yogurt. I need a fire truck," I said.

Bobby laughed.

"If you guys will excuse me, I think I'll go catch the news," Clay said after we'd helped him clear the plates.

Bobby turned to me after Clay left the room. "He doesn't seem like such a bad guy."

"He's worse than you think," I said.

Bobby thought about that for a minute. "Hey man, I'm really sorry," he said, lowering his voice. "What does he do—drink or beat you up or give your mom a hard time?"

"Nah, it's nothing like that."

"Well then, what's wrong with him? Why do you hate him so much?"

I could tell Bobby was waiting for an answer. But at first, I didn't know what to say. Why did I hate Clay?

Then, just like that, the answer occurred to me. "I hate him," I told Bobby, "because he's not my father."

Chapter Six

"I'm going to the library to load up on some new mysteries," Clay announced the next night. "I'll be back in about fifteen minutes."

I'd been to the library with Clay before, so I knew he'd be gone at least an hour. It takes him forever—and then some—to choose a book. First he studies the cover as if he's lost and it's a map; then he reads the author biography on the back of the book jacket; and when that's done, he reads the first page. Sometimes out loud, which is really embarrassing if you're with him. Even after he chooses a book, he goes back to the shelf at least two more times—just to make sure he didn't miss something or drop his library card.

I wasn't in the mood to watch TV or play on the computer. Our house, which usually cooled off when the sun went down, still felt like a hothouse. Which is fine if you're a tropical plant, but not so good if you're a kid. I needed air.

So I decided to go for a walk. A little stroll.

The street was deserted, and except for the light from the street lamps, it was completely dark. My only company was the crickets, who were chirping like mad. I wondered if they were trying to tell each other something. Maybe they had a feeling it was going to be a big night.

I wandered down the block toward the Levesques' house. The upstairs lights were on. I hadn't seen Patsy since the day she'd borrowed our X-Acto knife, and I wondered how she was doing. If I were less shy, I could call her up and ask. If it were Bobby, he'd have called her. Just like he invited himself for dinner. Anyway, I told myself, I'm sure I'll see Patsy around. There was something about her—and it wasn't just her looks—that made me want to get to know her better.

I was thinking about walking over to the park to see whether anyone was playing basketball when I noticed one of the side windows on the Levesques' house was wide open. All that was covering it was a mesh screen.

I walked over to get a better look. The whole time I was thinking about Patsy and the way her eyes crinkled when she smiled. Just as I'd thought, the window was open. Wide open. Someone could crawl right in—as long as he wasn't too big. Someone like me.

I started to play with the screen. The windows looked old and the screen was rusted at the bottom, so I figured it might be jammed, but it wasn't. It slid open noiselessly. Once it was open, it only took me a couple of seconds to slip inside.

I had to jump down to reach the floor. It was a good thing I was wearing my high-tops; it was also a good thing there was wall-to-wall carpeting or the Levesques might have heard me.

It took a minute for my eyes to adjust to the dark. I figured I was in the living room. Except for a couch and a glass coffee table, there wasn't much furniture.

Upstairs, someone was watching TV. I could hear the laugh track from a sitcom. I eyed the stairway at the far end of the hall. I wasn't into checking out rooms or furniture. I was interested in people—in families—and they were upstairs. But could I get to the second floor without anyone noticing?

Just then I heard a key in the front door. I'd assumed everyone was home, but I was wrong. My eyes darted around the room as I looked for a hiding place. The couch was tight against the wall, and the glass coffee table wasn't exactly an option. My best bet was a closet between the living room and dining room. I heard the doorknob turning. I dashed over to the closet, sneaked inside and shut the door behind me.

It's a good thing I'm not claustrophobic. It was the smallest closet I'd ever seen. They used it to store cleaning stuff, like brooms and a bucket. The smell of ammonia tickled my nose. I hoped I wouldn't sneeze.

The stairs to the second floor were just overhead, and I heard them creak as someone came down from upstairs.

"Is that you, Sylvain?" It was Patsy's mother. "You said you'd be home by eight." She didn't sound happy. I checked my watch—it was 8:37. It wasn't like Mr. Levesque was all that late. Why was she giving him a hard time?

She said something else, but she lowered her voice, and I couldn't make out what it was. I pressed my ear to the door so I'd be able to hear better.

"You were there again, weren't you?" she was saying.

Mr. Levesque didn't say anything. I heard them head down the hall. The layout was similar to our house, so I figured they were probably going to the kitchen. A refrigerator door opened, and I heard ice cubes tinkling into a glass.

I was surprised when out of nowhere I heard a whimpering sound—the kind of noise a dog makes when it's hurt. But I didn't think the Levesques had a dog. If they did, wouldn't I have seen them outside walking it by now? I strained to hear better. Now I heard a soft groaning sound. That was when I realized it had to be coming from a person.

It was Mrs. Levesque crying. What could she be so upset about?

"Don't make a scene, Annette," Mr. Levesque finally said. He paused for a couple of seconds before adding, "Patsy." He said it like it was a warning. Whatever they were discussing was something they didn't want Patsy to know about.

I heard Mrs. Levesque make a sniffling sound like she was blowing her nose.

"You have to stop. You're ruining us," she whispered.

Stop what? I wondered. What could Mr. Levesque be doing that would ruin his family?

"I won tonight," he told her. "I thought you'd be happy."

"I'd be happy if you worked a regular job. I'd be happy if you stopped gambling. I'd be happy if we could stop running away from all the people you owe money to."

So that was it. Mr. Levesque was a gambler. No wonder his wife was so upset.

"Okay," he said. "I'll stop. I promise."

Mrs. Levesque sighed. "How much did you win?"

"A thousand dollars."

Wow, I thought, a thousand dollars was like two years' worth of allowance. He won all that in just one night?

"That's nothing compared to what we owe," Mrs. Levesque said.

I heard the sound of more steps overhead. Patsy was coming downstairs. "Hey, Dad!" she called out, and I could hear her run over to him. "Come see the drawing I've been working on."

After the three of them went upstairs, I let five minutes go by before I left the closet. Partly, I wanted to be sure they wouldn't come back down. Partly, I needed to think. What I thought about was how there are some secrets you'd rather not know.

Chapter Seven

"Why did he do that?"

I was trying to watch a rerun of a NBA playoff game, but Clay kept interrupting with dumb questions.

"Why are they letting him take an extra turn?"

"He's got a free throw, you big idiot."

I didn't really say that. But I wanted to. The guy's totally clueless when it comes to B-ball.

It was the Pistons versus the Lakers and the game was really heating up. I dug my fingertips into the couch. Not because I was anxious about the game. More because I was sure Clay was about to ask me another dumb question.

"That's called an assist, right?"

I was thinking about telling him he could assist me by shutting up, when the screen went blank. My first thought was that the picture tube had blown. But then this lady news reporter with wavy black hair suddenly appeared on the screen. At least the TV was still working. "We regret having to interrupt our regularly scheduled programming to bring you this news alert," she said in a tense-sounding voice. "We have breaking news about Montreal's home invader—news we believe our viewers need to know."

"News we believe our viewers need to know," I said, imitating the woman's voice. Why couldn't they break the news after the game?

"Shh," Clay said, without looking at me. "This sounds serious."

"Montreal Daily News—the city's premier news station—has learned that the home invader struck again two hours ago. Preliminary reports indicate the home invader broke into a home in Monkland Village in Notre-Dame-de-Grâce at about 4:15 PM."

"Monkland Village," Clay said, whistling. "This guy's in our neck of the woods now."

"It is still not clear how the home invader managed to gain entrance into the house, a gray brick bungalow near the corner of Sherbrooke Street West and Madison Avenue," continued the broadcaster.

You could tell from the glassy look in the reporter's eyes that she was reading off a TelePrompTer. "What is clear," she added, "is that the home invader ambushed the house's residents—a thirty-four-year-old woman and her six-year-old daughter—tied them up and ransacked the home, stealing a portable computer and DVD player, as well as items of jewelry. The home invader is believed to have escaped on foot.

"Both victims are in hospital, where they are being treated for trauma. But Montreal

Daily News has managed to obtain an interview with a neighbor."

The neighbor had white hair and a long face like a horse. "I had no idea anything was wrong until the husband came home at around six. We were chatting while he was waiting for his wife to answer the door. He started to get nervous when she didn't come. She always answers the door. In the end, he let himself in. About five minutes later, I heard sirens. He must have phoned the police. They took the woman and the little girl to the hospital. They're nice, quiet people. I don't know why someone would do something like this." The old guy's face was turning red, and he was starting to sound out of breath. You could tell he wasn't used to talking so much.

I couldn't help shivering when the camera focused on the street where the family lived. I recognized the huge weeping willow tree at the corner. I passed that corner every day on my way to the community center.

The reporter's face popped back on the screen. "Montreal Daily News—the city's premier news station—"

"Don't you wish they'd stop saying that?" I asked Clay.

"—now brings you Professor Andrew Tourneau, a professor of criminology at McGill University. What can you tell us, Professor Tourneau, about the kind of person who'd invade homes? Who'd take pleasure in terrorizing innocent citizens?" continued the reporter.

Professor Tourneau looked exactly as you'd expect a professor to look. He had a big mop of messy hair like Albert Einstein's, wire-rimmed glasses, and he was wearing a tweed blazer. "You have hit the nail on the head, Miss," he told the reporter. "A home invader is someone who takes pleasure in terrorizing others. The home invader may be motivated partly by greed—after all, he steals computers and stereo equipment and jewelry—but I'd venture to say the home invader gets his real thrills from having power over helpless individuals. From watching them cower in fear."

"When you say 'he,'" the reporter interrupted the professor, "are you saying you believe the home invader is a male?"

"Forgive me," Professor Tourneau said. "I stand corrected. I understand the police have not yet determined the sex of the home invader. However, according to the literature, most home invaders are male."

"Thank you, Professor Tourneau." The reporter reached out to shake Tourneau's hand. "Before we end our special broadcast, we have a final guest: Constable Marie Leduc, a police spokesperson. Constable Leduc, I believe you have some tips for our viewers about how to keep the home invader from entering their homes."

I could tell from the way the police officer was tapping her pen on the table that she was nervous. It had been over a month and the police still hadn't caught the home invader. That didn't exactly make them look good. "Despite the hot weather," Constable Leduc said, "we are urging Montrealers to keep their windows completely sealed." I thought about how the Levesques had left their window open, with only the screen to cover it. Then, as if she was reading my mind, Constable Leduc added, "Screens do not provide sufficient protection. We also recommend that homeowners ensure all doors to their houses are properly locked. We've even heard reports of some individuals accidentally leaving their keys in their locks."

"Imagine doing something like that," Clay said.

"People do it all the time," I told him.

I could feel Clay watching me.

"We're not here to create fear in our viewers, but Madame Leduc, could you tell us what to do should the home invader make his—or her—way into our homes?"

Constable Leduc looked up into the camera. "The main thing we recommend is that you cooperate with the home invader." She stopped to clear her throat. "The home invader is armed and dangerous."

"Holy Toledo," Clay said.

"Holy what?"

"Toledo. It's a city in Ohio. But it was named after an old Spanish city. El Greco painted it." For a second, I thought Clay had distracted himself by telling me about some old painter and that he'd forgotten all about the home invader. But then he surprised me by getting back on topic. "You know, Josh," he said, "we better make sure all the windows are sealed."

"If you didn't smoke up the kitchen, we wouldn't need to keep opening them."

Clay ignored my comment. "If the home invader wanted power," he said, "he should've gone into politics."

"Maybe he's just curious."

Clay looked at me. "What do you mean?"

I looked out the window toward the other houses that lined our street. "Maybe he's curious about other people. About what kind of lives they have."

"How would you know?" Clay asked.

"I wouldn't. Let's watch basketball."

Only then there were commercials: one for detergent, another for guard dogs. By the time they were over, so was the game.

Chapter Eight

There were thirty seconds left. It was the fourth quarter and the score was tied at forty-eight. We were playing another camp team from Montreal's East End. They had the ball. Their point guard—a blond guy with wire-rimmed glasses—was dribbling up the court. I watched him eye the clock.

"Isolation!" he yelled, calling a play. All the players on his team rushed to the right side of the court. Which left just him and me one-on-one. For a split second our eyes met. Then I looked down at his hips; I knew they'd tell me the direction he'd be going in.

Basketball's a bit like poker. Bluffing the other guy is part of the game. When he started dribbling left, I had this feeling he was about to spin right again—and he did. Then he faded away from sixteen feet. It was a beautiful shot.

They were ahead of us by two points now. Six seconds remained on the scoreboard. We still had a chance. A lot can happen in six seconds.

Just then our coach called a twenty-second time-out. "Just focus," he told us. I wiped the sweat from my forehead and tried to catch my breath. My heart was beating like crazy.

Bobby inbounded the ball to me. I looked up at the clock as I started dribbling up court. Four seconds.

One of the guys on my team was setting a pick on my right side. I crossed left to right, stopping just outside the arc. That left me open for the three-point shot. The shot that would win us the game.

I'd just released the ball from my finger-tips when the buzzer sounded.

"He got it off in time!" I heard our coach's booming voice, though it sounded like it was coming from far away. My eyes were focused on the ball. I watched as it bounced off the left side of the rim, then hit the right.

"Yes!" I whispered under my breath, willing the ball to sink into the net. I could practically hear the swishing sound it would make. The ball rolled once around the rim, then popped out and fell to the ground.

The guys on the other team were high-fiving each other. I wished I could disappear. I felt even worse when a couple of guys on my team slapped my shoulder. Consolation slaps.

What really put me over the edge was when the coach pulled me aside and said, "You did your best, Josh. That's what counts."

"I can't stand that crap about how doing your best counts more than winning," I told Bobby on the way home. We'd hardly spo-ken since we left the community center, and I was grateful he hadn't mentioned the game. I knew he must've been disappointed too, but at least he wasn't the one responsible for botching things up.

"I know what you mean," he said quietly.

"Sometimes doing your best just isn't good enough," I muttered.

Bobby adjusted the strap on his sports bag and then turned to me. "It was a tough shot," he said.

"Don't go making excuses for me." I hadn't meant to snap; that was just how it came out.

Bobby shrugged. Which was pretty much where our conversation ended that afternoon.

Sometimes the best time to break into a house is when you're doing something else. I was just walking, thinking about how I didn't feel like going home, and picturing the basketball popping out of the rim and dropping to the ground, when a gruff voice interrupted my thoughts. "Take this!" the voice said.

Next thing I knew, someone was passing me this huge cardboard box. It wasn't like

I had much choice—the box was pressing against my chest—so I took it. Bending a little at the knees, I tried to balance the box in my arms. The thing was so big I could hardly see over it. Plus it was heavy.

Somehow I'd gotten myself in the middle of someone's move. If I'd been paying more attention, I'd have crossed the street when I saw the moving truck. But I'd been too busy replaying the game in my head.

"Come on, move it!" the gruff voice commanded. To my left, I noticed a bald guy with sunburned shoulders carrying a box into a nearby apartment building. I followed him.

The door to the lobby had been propped open. The building smelled like cabbage. I followed the bald guy up the stairs to a corner apartment on the second floor. When he dropped his box on the wood floor and turned around to go back downstairs, I tried to duck behind my box. But he saw me. The weird thing was he didn't seem the least bit surprised. All he did was make a grunting noise, and then he headed back down.

I could've left right then. But I didn't. Instead I slipped behind the closest door. With the rooms empty, except for boxes, it was hard to tell what room I was in. The bedroom, I decided.

"I can't believe this is happening!" someone said. Looking around the edge of the door, I could see a guy walking out of what seemed to be the kitchen—a small, sunny room at the back of the apartment—his arm around a girl's waist. They looked like they were in their early twenties. He was wearing a red bandana; she had long, dark hair that she wore in a braid down her back. It was tied at the bottom with a red ribbon.

"I know," the girl said in a breathless voice. "Me and you. Our first apartment. I can't believe it either."

Just my luck, I thought. Bad enough I have to put up with Mom and Clay, but now I've walked in on another pair of lovebirds. I hoped these two weren't about to start making out. After all, the moving guys would be back any minute with more stuff.

"This is so cool," the guy said. "Our own

place." Then he leaned in like he was about to kiss her. Luckily the moving guys showed up right then. There were three of them now, but only two were carrying boxes.

"We're all done," the empty-handed one announced. He was the one who had handed me the box outside. "That'll be two hundred and fifty bucks," he told the couple.

"You guys were great," the girl said. "Thanks so much for everything." She took an envelope from her pocket and handed it to the boss.

The guy shut the door behind the moving men. "Here's to our life together," he said. He was carrying two plastic bottles of spring water. He gave one to his girlfriend; then they toasted each other. Pretty corny, if you ask me.

"What now?" The girl looked up at her boyfriend. When she giggled, I started getting nervous.

"We unpack," the guy said. I nearly sighed out loud.

He turned toward the room I was in and reached for the closest box, sliding it over toward him. I was standing in the doorway, only partially hidden by the door.

Our eyes met. When he looked at me, he didn't seem afraid. Just curious. "What are you doing here, kid?" he asked, getting up from his spot on the floor and opening the door all the way.

I didn't say a thing.

The girlfriend made enough noise for all of us, though. "Call the police!" she shrieked. "It's the home invader!"

Chapter Nine

The guy was standing so close I could hear him breathing and see the beads of sweat trickling down his neck. "I'm not the home invader," I said.

"Who are you then?" he asked me.

"I…I was just walking by when the movers handed me a box." I knew it sounded lame, but it was all I could think of. Besides, it's what happened.

The girl had backed up all the way to the window, and her face, which had turned almost white when she first saw me, was beginning to get its color back. "It's really creepy the way he was watching us, John," she said, her voice shaking.

John looked into my eyes. "Did you take anything?"

"No way," I told him, opening my hands to show him they were empty. "Besides," I added, "there's nothing to take. Everything's packed."

"He has a point there, Clarisse," John said, turning around to face her.

"We should call the police just the same. He invaded our home," Clarisse insisted. Her voice was high-pitched and whiny.

How could John stand her? Then he said something that surprised me. "I know you're stressed out," he told Clarisse. "But everything will be okay. We've got each other, right?"

When Clarisse smiled back at him, she didn't seem so upset anymore.

If John hadn't been blocking my way, I could've made a run for it. Careful to keep my eyes on the floor so they wouldn't know what I was thinking, I tried to study the room. We were too high up for me to jump out a window, but if I could find some way to distract them, I might be able to run out the door and downstairs to the street.

"Can't you just let me go?" I asked John. I knew there was no sense in talking to Clarisse; she'd made up her mind about me. In fact she was rummaging through her purse, probably looking for her cell phone so she could turn me in. I knew I was running out of time.

"He didn't take anything." This time, when John turned back to Clarisse, I made a run for it. Getting out of the apartment and past all those boxes was a bit like dribbling around those orange cones in the gym.

I could hear John stumbling behind me. And I could hear Clarisse shrieking on the telephone: "I'm calling to report a home invasion!"

I flew down the stairs and out the front door, which no one had bothered to close.

I was trying to decide whether to keep

running or find someplace to hide when I felt someone grab my shoulder.

"Not so fast, young man!" a voice said. I didn't need to see the uniform to know he was a cop.

"I got here as soon as I could, officer."

I could hear Clay's voice from behind the door. He sounded nervous—like he was the one who'd got caught doing something wrong.

They'd hauled me down to the local police station. The worst part was sitting in the back of the police cruiser. When we stopped at a light, I made the mistake of looking into the car next to us. Patsy was in the passenger seat; her mom was at the wheel. I turned away the second I realized it was Patsy, but it was too late. She'd spotted me. She looked like she was about to wave, but then, all of a sudden, she turned away. I figured she didn't want to embarrass me.

At least they didn't throw me into a cell. Instead they made me sit in this little room that felt like the waiting room at the doctor's—only there were no magazines or coughing kids. It wasn't anything like on TV. Nobody read me my rights or asked if I wanted a lawyer.

One cop brought me a Coke and asked me to tell her what I'd been doing in the apartment. "It just sort of happened," I told her and explained about the moving truck.

"Have you done this kind of thing before?" she asked, without taking her eyes off mine.

I took a quick breath. "Never," I lied.

Now I could hear her talking to Clay, saying that couple had decided not to press charges, that the police were going to allow me to go home, but that I had to be under Clay's constant supervision. Just my luck, I thought.

"Have you considered taking him to a family counselor?" I heard the cop ask Clay. I tapped the arms of my chair while I waited for Clay to say something.

"We thought he was doing okay," he said at last. "We just figured he was having some adjustment difficulties. Getting-used-to-the-new-stepfather kind of stuff." As if anyone could ever get used to Clay.

"I know what it's like," the cop said with a sigh. "My boyfriend has a son. He's only six, but the kid's impossible. God knows what he'll be like at fifteen."

"Put on your seatbelt," Clay told her. "You're in for a rough ride."

Gimme a break, I thought. The woman's in for a rough ride? What about the kid? Let's just hope his dad's girlfriend is a little more normal than Clay.

"So what the hell were you thinking?" Clay asked me when we were in his car.

"I wasn't thinking anything." Somehow I'd expected him to be nicer. He was obviously pissed with me.

"You must've been thinking something," he insisted.

That's when I blew. "Okay," I told him. "If you really want to know what I was thinking—here it is. I was thinking how I screwed up at basketball today. I was thinking how I didn't want to go home and find you lounging on the couch or destroying our house. I was thinking how I wished I lived someplace else—anywhere else—as long as you weren't there."

I stopped to catch my breath. It was the most I'd ever said to Clay in all the time I'd known him.

I was a little surprised when he pulled the car over to the side of the road. When he turned to face me, I had this overwhelming urge to jump out right then and there. Then he leaned over and put his hand over mine. I flinched. Clay must've noticed because he backed right off.

"Listen to me, Josh," he said. "This isn't what anyone would call an ideal situation. You're stuck with me—and I'm stuck with you, and there's very little either of us can do about it. The one thing we have in common is that we both love your mom."

I flinched again. My mom would have a bird when she found out what I'd done. "You're not going to tell her, are you?" I asked quietly. I slid my fingers along the door handle while I waited for Clay to say something.

But all he said was, "Get your hand off the door handle."

When the phone rang, I rushed to answer it. Clay got to it before me. I knew it would be Mom. She'd phoned every night at exactly seven o'clock.

The conversation started with Clay asking about Gramps. They were going to release him from hospital in a couple more days. From what I could tell, Mom was having more trouble dealing with Gramma. She wouldn't leave Gramps' bedside even when it was time for visitors to go home.

My heart started pounding when the conversation switched to how things were going at home. Mom would freak out when she heard about my run-in with the police—and she's not a lot of fun when she freaks out. She's also the type who believes in punishments. I wondered what she'd make me do when she found out. I had a feeling docking my allowance wouldn't satisfy her. She'd come up with something crueler. Something that would involve Clay.

I kept waiting for him to bring up what had happened. Only he didn't. "I'll put him on," Clay said, passing me the phone after he'd been on for nearly ten minutes. "Then you can ask him yourself."

I took the receiver from his hands. "How are you doing, Mom? How's Gramps?" I was hoping she wouldn't be able to tell from my voice that something was wrong. She's like a bloodhound when it comes to sniffing out trouble.

"Things are under control here, honey," she said. Mom sounded tired, but not suspicious. I relaxed a little. "I just wanted to know how you and Clay are getting on," she said. "Are you two finally bonding?"

I looked at Clay. He'd put on the maroon housecoat when we got home from the police station. His fingers were stained with red and blue paint. "Yeah, I guess you could say we're...bonding." The words stuck in my throat. But it was only when Clay started smiling—this huge, goofy smile—that I really regretted saying them.

There was one more thing I didn't really feel like saying, only I knew I had to.

"Thanks," I told Clay after dinner. We were standing at the sink; he was washing, I was drying. "For not mentioning anything to Mom about...you know."

He passed me a pot, then lifted his chin toward the living room window. "See what I see?"

A police cruiser was driving by. It slowed down as it passed our house. I thought about Patsy and the puzzled look she'd given me when she'd spotted me earlier that day.

"It's not the first cop car that's driven by tonight," Clay said. "I think they're trailing you. Look," he added, "I decided not to tell your mom about what happened. She's got enough on her mind already. But there's one condition."

"What's that?" I asked him.

"I figure a guy like you knows a thing or two about invading homes. I want you to help me catch the real home invader. God knows the police aren't having much luck. And if we can figure out who it is, the cops might just leave you alone."

Chapter Ten

When Clay suggested we go to the bagel shop for breakfast on Saturday morning, I figured I didn't have much choice. It's not that I don't like the bagel shop. They do their scrambled eggs just right—not too drippy—and they make their bagels in a wood-burning oven at the back of the store. What I wasn't in the mood for was Clay.

There is one thing I do have against the bagel shop, though. We were having breakfast there when Mom and Clay announced they were getting married. It's a wonder I can still eat scrambled eggs.

Clay was sitting across from me now, tapping his foot on the floor. I wanted to tell him to cut it out, but then I figured I owed him one for not ratting me out to Mom.

Just after we gave the waitress our order, Clay pulled this little sketchpad and a pencil from his jacket pocket. "Okay," he said, opening the sketchpad to a blank page. "Tell me everything you know about breaking into houses—everything you've observed."

"I only did it that one time."

Clay looked up from the sketchpad. "Level with me," he said. "Tell me what you know. One thing I've learned from reading mysteries is that solving one is a lot like painting. It's all about the details."

I was thinking about that when the waitress reappeared with our food. Clay moved his sketchpad to the edge of the table.

I took a bite of my bagel. "Well," I told him, "basically, you need to watch for ways to get inside. You know, open doors, window screens, garages…" That made me think of Patsy. I wondered what was up with her—and how her family was doing.

Clay nodded. "It is just like painting," he said, waving his fork in the air like he was a conductor and the fork was a baton. I hoped he wouldn't jab someone with it. "A painter needs to see what other people miss. The dew on the grass first thing in the morning. The way some old people shuffle when they walk. A spider's web in the corner of a—"

I couldn't take it anymore. "Look," I said, cutting Clay off, "how exactly are you planning to find the home invader?"

Clay put his fork back down on his plate. "First," he said, "I need to understand how the home invader thinks. Once I know that, I imagine the rest will fall into place."

He made it sound so easy that, for a second, I believed him. But a second after that I went back to thinking he was a nut. Still, I had to tell him something—even if it was just to get him to stop jabbering about all the stuff artists have to notice. "You know," I told him, "a home invader might leave clues."

Clay reached for his sketchpad. "Like what?" he asked.

"After a rainfall, footprints in the mud. Ladders where they shouldn't be. Scaffolding on the side of a building. Flowers that look like they've been trampled on."

Clay nodded. I watched as he used his pencil to draw a tiny footprint at the top of the page. He made scratching sounds as he worked. He added some dark lines and, presto—it looked like mud.

I was about to tell him I didn't know he could draw real stuff—and not just blobs—when Patsy walked into the bagel shop. She was heading for the counter at the back where they sell fresh bagels.

Clay must've seen her too. "Hey, isn't that Patricia from down the street?"

"Patsy," I corrected him.

She must've heard me say her name, because she turned in our direction.

"Patsy!" Clay called out before I could stop him. "How are you doing, neighbor?"

She paused for a second, then came over to our table.

Clay stood up. I thought he was trying to be polite, but it turned out he had to go to the bathroom. He tapped Patsy's elbow when he passed her. "Nice to see you," he said.

That left just me and her. For a second, neither of us said anything. Patsy was the one who broke the silence. "I saw you the other day," she said. She'd put her hands in the pockets of her shorts, and she was shifting from one foot to the other.

"I know."

"What were you doing in a cop car anyway?"

I stared down at my plate. What would Patsy think if she knew the truth—that I got a weird thrill from spying on other people, including her? "It was a case of mistaken identity," I said when I looked back up at her. "I'm thinking of suing the police, you know—for tarnishing my reputation. For treating me like a common criminal. I mean, what are people supposed to think? Especially people who saw me on my way down to the station."

"People who know you would never think you were a common criminal."

"Thanks," I said, smiling up at her.

"An uncommon one, maybe," Patsy said, smiling back.

I laughed. The thing was, Patsy had no idea how right she was. "So what have you been up to?" I asked her. I figured now was a good time to change the subject.

"Oh, you know, unpacking, getting my room arranged. I met this girl, Tasha, who goes to Royal Crest. She said she knows you. We've been hanging out."

"Tasha's okay," I told her. "So how are your mom and dad? Getting settled in okay too?"

Patsy shrugged her shoulders. "I don't know about you, but my parents just keep getting weirder and weirder."

I wanted to know more, but Clay interrupted us. "You two should do something together sometime. Why don't you make some plans with her, Josh?" he said, pulling his chair out from the table. Then he clapped me on the shoulder.

I felt my face get hot. Why did he have to be such a jerk?

Patsy took her hands out of her pockets. "Well, I'd better get some bagels," she said. Then she tilted her chin toward me. "It'd be great to do something sometime…" she said.

"I—I'll come by your house."

Clay waited for Patsy to walk to the counter at the back. Then he leaned over and nudged my elbow. "You're some smooth operator," he said.

I gritted my teeth. Then I closed my eyes and tried to remember what my life was like before he came along and ruined it.

Chapter Eleven

We ran errands after breakfast. We returned books to the library, dropped off clothes at the dry cleaner, shopped for groceries. I had to come since I was under you-know-who's supervision. I tried not to notice the cop car parked by the grocery store, but when I got out of the car, I felt eyes on me. Clay must've noticed too, because he put his arm around my shoulders, only I shook it off.

I unpacked the groceries. If I hadn't, Clay would've left them out in the hallway all week.

"I'm gonna have a little nap," he announced, stretching his arms. "Part of my plan to catch the home invader. I read about this study that says people think better when they're lying down. What are your plans, Josh?"

I hadn't counted on having unsupervised time. "Ahh, I guess I'll play on the computer, send Mom an e-mail."

"Say hi from me. Don't worry. No mushy stuff. Just hi." Clay grabbed a mystery from the pile on the living room table. Was that also part of his plan for catching the home invader?

I had a lot of junk mail to delete. After that I wrote Mom. I could hear the steady drone of Clay's snoring coming from the living room: a quick inhalation followed by a loud wheezing sound. The guy even snored weird.

Taking small steps so the stairs wouldn't creak, I went downstairs. Clay's mouth was open. The book was lying facedown on his lap. If he woke up now, I'd say I was getting a snack. Maybe he wanted a bowl of ice cream too.

Outside the sky was as blue as a robin's egg. I could imagine my gramma saying how it's criminal to stay inside on a sunny day. Gramma was right. I went over to the window and peered up and down the street. No cop cars.

I grabbed my basketball. Usually I'd have dribbled in the hallway, but I didn't want to do anything that might wake Clay up—and ruin my plans for the afternoon.

I headed down the street toward Patsy's house. I pictured myself ringing her doorbell. She'd invite me in; her mom would offer me a cold drink. Then I'd ask Patsy on a date. "Wanna catch a movie with me?" I whispered to myself. I was pretty sure she'd say yes. Otherwise she wouldn't have acted so friendly at the bagel shop.

By the time I got to Patsy's, I wasn't feeling as confident. What if my voice squeaked? What if I blushed the way I sometimes did? What if she said no?

Mrs. Levesque was trimming a hedge at the side of the house. I watched her lay her shears on the grass. Then she stood up and clapped her hands to loosen the dirt from her fingers. "Hi, Josh," she called out when she spotted me walking by. "Going to play basketball?"

I bounced my ball on the sidewalk. I considered telling her I was about to drop in on Patsy, but somehow I couldn't. "Yup, gonna shoot some hoops," I mumbled.

"Have fun," she said as she adjusted her sun hat. That's when I noticed the side window was open again. This time there wasn't even a screen covering it. Hadn't the Levesques been watching the news? I nearly said something, but then, at the last second, I changed my mind.

When I got to the park, I shot a few hoops, but I kept thinking about that window. Instead of shooting hoops, I went back to the Levesques' house. Now there was no sign of Mrs. Levesque. I walked over to the window. It was still wide open—teasing me, like an invitation to a party I really wanted to go to.

Sometimes it felt like I was destined to be a home invader. And why fight destiny?

I peered in through the window to make sure the coast was clear. There was no sign of anyone on the first floor. So I hoisted myself in through the window and jumped down to the floor.

Instantly I felt the familiar rush of pleasure. Watching people when they didn't know I was there gave me a kind of high. Now was my chance to learn more about what was going on with the Levesques. Once I knew, I wouldn't need to come back. At least not like this.

"Patsy!" Mrs. Levesque's voice called from the basement. "Can you help me carry this planter out to the yard?"

"Can't it wait?" Patsy shouted from upstairs.

"No, it can't!" Mrs. Levesque insisted.

"Okay, then, I'm coming!"

I knew that meant Patsy would be coming down the stairs any second. So I ducked behind the living room door.

When Patsy rushed past me, her soapy smell lingered in the air. "There are a few more things you can help me with now that you're here," I heard Mrs. Levesque say. Patsy moaned.

I stepped out from behind the door and walked over to the coffee table. On it were several framed photographs of the Levesques. Patsy and her parents lying in beach chairs. Another photo of the three of them with Mickey Mouse, probably taken at Disneyland. In the photos, at least, they looked like the perfect family—smiling and relaxed. But then I thought about the way I'd seen Mr. and Mrs. Levesque arguing, and Mr. Levesque's gambling problem. Maybe there was no such thing as a perfect family.

I had to stop looking at the photos when I heard Patsy and her mom coming up from the basement. This time my best bet seemed to be the utility closet. I sneaked in and crouched down between the bucket and brooms.

"Patsy, how about helping me mop the floor?" Mrs. Levesque asked. My heart started beating hard inside my chest. What would Patsy think if she found me? I inched back a little further into the closet. There wasn't much room, but I managed to hide behind what looked like a painter's drop cloth.

"I wanted to go over to Tasha's," Patsy muttered.

"We'll just do the kitchen floor then."

I got another whiff of Patsy's soapy scent when she reached into the closet for the bucket. I was curious to hear what else Patsy and her mom would have to say to each other, but with the kitchen tap running, I couldn't make out their voices.

I let myself rest on a corner of the drop cloth. Between getting caught by the police and dealing with Clay, things had been pretty crazy the last couple of days. Who'd have guessed a guy would finally get to relax inside somebody else's closet?

I must've dozed off, because when I woke up, I had a crick in my neck. Uh-oh, I thought, what's Clay gonna think? It felt like I'd been asleep for a while. I saw that the mop and bucket were back at the front of the closet. I was about to push open the door when I heard voices.

I pressed my ear to the door to hear better.

"Who are you?" Mrs. Levesque was asking. Her voice sounded higher than usual.

"Just do what I say," a gruff voice insisted. "I've got a knife."

Yikes, I thought, what's going on here? I maneuvered my body so that I got a little closer to the front of the closet.

"Do what he says, Annette." It was Mr. Levesque. From the sound of it, he was standing in the hallway, just outside the utility closet.

It had to be the home invader. The real home invader. If my heart had raced before, you should have heard it now. For a moment, I was afraid the others might hear it.

"Sit right here."

"Don't hurt me!" Mrs. Levesque whimpered as the home invader dragged her to the other side of the living room.

"Listen to him, Annette." Mr. Levesque's voice sounded a little farther away now. He was probably following his wife into the living room.

Where was Patsy? Had she left the house while I was asleep?

I thought about leaping out of the closet right then. But the home invader had a knife. I had only one advantage: that he didn't know I was there. For now, the best thing to do was wait—and try to come up with a plan.

I heard a loud tearing noise. It sounded like tape. He must be tying up the Levesques.

"Tell me where your valuables are and nobody will get hurt."

"M…my jewelry is in my n…nightstand; so is the c…cash," Mrs. Levesque stammered.

"What about laptops?"

"I have one in my briefcase. It's by the door," Mr. Levesque said. "Over there." I could tell he was doing his best to cooperate with the home invader.

I heard the home invader snap open the briefcase. I thought he'd go upstairs for the jewelry, but instead he went back over to the Levesques. I heard muffled noises and the sound of more tape. "Don't…" Mrs. Levesque said in a pleading voice.

Now I had managed to inch close enough to the front of the closet that I could open it a crack and see out. I pressed gently on the door so they wouldn't hear me. Mrs. Levesque's eyes were bulging with fear. I thought she was about to cry, but then her husband gave her a stern look. I watched as he mouthed the words "Stay calm!"

All I could see of the home invader was his back. He had broad shoulders, and despite the hot weather he was wearing a long-sleeved sweatshirt. He gagged Mrs. Levesque; next he stuffed what looked like an old washcloth into Mr. Levesque's mouth. Just watching made my mouth feel dry and sore.

Just then I heard footsteps overhead. Patsy. So she was home after all. Now she was coming downstairs, humming loudly, the way people do when they're wearing a headset. I watched the home invader's back as he headed toward the stairs. Don't hurt her, I thought to myself.

"Why are you wearing that stupid mask, Dad?" Patsy asked. "It's not Halloween."

"You're right; it's not."

That's when Patsy screamed, but only for a second.

"You wouldn't want to scare the neighbors, now, would you?" the home invader asked. He must have grabbed hold of her then, because I heard the sounds of a scuffle. A moment later, I watched as he led Patsy to another chair. When she reached out her foot to trip him, the home invader pulled out his knife. Its long blade glistened threateningly.

My breath caught in my throat. "Don't make me hurt you," the home invader growled as he tied Patsy up and gagged her.

I had to stop myself from gasping when the home invader finally turned around and I saw his face. He was wearing a skeleton mask, with drops of blood dripping from between the glow-in-the-dark bones. That's when I knew for sure the home invader was no regular thief. A guy who broke into people's houses wearing that kind of mask had to be as interested in scaring them as he was in stealing their stuff. Suddenly I remembered what the professor had said during the TV interview.

Home invaders wanted to have power over helpless people.

He rushed upstairs. I could hear him pulling open doors and drawers, growing louder and more frantic as he searched.

Then he rushed back downstairs. "There's no jewelry or cash!" he shouted as he came into the living room.

He tugged the cloth from Mrs. Levesque's mouth. The skin around her mouth was red and swollen. "It's next to the bed," she said, her voice shaking and her eyes beginning to pool with tears. "I promise."

Patsy squirmed in her seat. I could tell that if she'd been able to, she'd have gotten up and jumped the home invader. But when I thought of his knife, I decided it was a good thing Patsy was tied up.

Mr. Levesque tried to say something. The home invader pulled the towel from his mouth too. "Annette…" This time I thought Mr. Levesque was about to cry. His voice, which had been strong until now, suddenly dropped to a whisper. "I spent the cash…and sold the jewelry."

Chapter Twelve

"What do you mean you sold the jewelry?" Mrs. Levesque didn't sound scared anymore; she sounded angry. Really angry.

"I'm sorry." Mr. Levesque dropped his eyes to the floor.

Now Patsy's eyes were darting back and forth between her parents. You could tell she was trying to make sense of their conversation.

The home invader threw his hands up

into the air. "What is this? Some kind of bad reality TV?"

Mrs. Levesque ignored him. Instead she focused on her husband. "You told me it was over, Sylvain. You told me things would change when we moved here."

"I tried, Annette…believe me, I tried."

Now Mrs. Levesque turned to the home invader. "He gambles. Now he's gambled away my jewelry. My grandmother's jewelry." Her voice shook.

Patsy's eyes looked like they were going to pop out of her head. Her cheeks were puffed up too, because of the gag in her mouth. I had the feeling this was the first she'd heard about her dad's gambling problem.

Patsy cringed when the home invader dropped to his knees in front of her. "I'll take this," he said, snatching her iPod from out of her pocket. Then he looked back at Mrs. Levesque. "You have silverware? Or did he sell that too?"

"It's in the kitchen," Mrs. Levesque said. "Second set of drawers to the left of the sink. At least it was there last time I checked," she added, giving her husband an accusing look.

"It's there," Mr. Levesque said in a hoarse voice.

As soon as the home invader got to the kitchen, I stepped out of the closet, carrying the metal bucket. My legs felt wobbly but at least now I had a plan. Well, sort of a plan anyway. Catching the home invader, solving a mystery, making a painting—they were all about details.

I raised a finger to my mouth. If the home invader found me now, he'd tie me up too, and then I wouldn't be of much use to the Levesques.

Patsy's eyes bulged. I could tell I had frightened her, but there wasn't anything I could do about it then. Right now, every second counted.

I could hear the home invader pulling open kitchen drawers. Then I heard the clatter of silverware as he emptied it into a bag.

If only I had a little more time. In the end, it was Mrs. Levesque who helped me out. "There's grocery money too. Not a lot, but you can have it if you'll go away and leave us alone," she called out so the home invader would hear her. "It's in the back pantry in a peanut butter jar."

The home invader whistled. "That's what I like," he called out. "Cooperation!"

I held the bucket by the handle, careful not to let it bump into anything. It wasn't exactly a lethal weapon, but it was all I had.

I took a deep breath and tiptoed toward the kitchen, keeping as close as possible to the wall. Like before, all I could see was the home invader's back. He was crouched on the floor, rummaging through the pantry and making grunting noises as he searched for the peanut butter jar. The handle of the knife jutted out of his side pocket.

I willed him not to turn around. Just give me a few more seconds, I thought. This time I couldn't hesitate.

I was so close I could smell him. I swung the pail with every ounce of strength I had, aiming right for the middle of the thin white elastic that was holding his skeleton mask in place.

He yelled as he tumbled over, his face to the ground. He was sprawled on the tile floor; his arms and legs were twitching. The bump on the back of his head was already as big as an egg. How long did I have before he regained consciousness? My fingers shook as I slid the knife out of his pocket. Then I raced back to the living room.

First I used the knife to cut the tape on Mr. Levesque's wrists and ankles. "Phone the police," I told him as I began freeing Mrs. Levesque and Patsy. The electrical tape had left red welts on their wrists and ankles. When I took the gag from Patsy's mouth, she started to cough. I hoped the noise wouldn't wake up the home invader.

In the background, I heard Mr. Levesque whispering on the phone.

Mostly, of course, I was listening for sounds in the kitchen. For now, all I heard was the steady drip of the Levesques' leaky faucet. With the knife in one hand, I grabbed what was left of the roll of electrical tape.

Patsy and her parents followed me back into the kitchen.

"Quick!" I said, keeping my voice low. "We need to drag him someplace where we can tie him up."

"The table!" Patsy said.

Together the four of us managed to drag the home invader over to the table. His mask was half off now, so we could see a bit of his face. It was badly sunburned and he had a thin moustache and small beard. He looked like a regular guy.

Using the long strips of tape Patsy handed me, I tied his wrists to the table legs. If he wanted to go anywhere, he'd have to take the table with him.

Suddenly he moaned. Then he opened one bloodshot eye. I lifted the knife into the air so he'd see I had it. "Don't make me use this," I said. I hoped he wouldn't notice my voice was shaking.

He moaned again when he heard the sirens. Mrs. Levesque let the cops in, while Patsy, her dad and I stayed in the kitchen with the home invader. His eyes were closed again, but he seemed to be breathing normally.

Four cops rushed into the kitchen, their hands on their holsters. "This young man managed to subdue him," Mr. Levesque said, clapping me on the shoulder. One of the cops loosened the home invader's hands from the table leg. At the same time, another one clasped a pair of handcuffs around the home invader's wrists.

I recognized the last cop. It was the woman from the police station—the one who'd complained about her boyfriend's kid. "What are you doing here?" she asked, her eyebrows arching as she spoke. "Your stepfather's supposed to be supervising you."

"I guess he's not doing a very good job," a voice said. I didn't have to turn around to know it was Clay. He was standing in the hallway, his cowlick sticking up. For the first time ever, I was glad to see him. Well, kind of glad, anyhow.

"What *were* you doing here?" Patsy wanted to know after the police had escorted the home invader from the Levesques' house. We were standing on the front balcony. Clay was inside, chatting with Patsy's parents.

I shrugged my shoulders. "Are you sure you really want to know?"

"Of course I do," Patsy said.

"I don't want you to think I'm a freak," I whispered.

I thought Patsy might turn away, but she didn't. "Look," she said, "whatever it is, you can tell me."

"The thing is," I said as I looked up into her eyes, "I'm kind of a home invader myself."

Chapter Thirteen

"No," Patsy said, blocking my hand when I tried to reach into my pocket for money. "I want to pay for both of us."

"No way," I told her. "Next time." I wanted her to know I hoped there'd be a next time.

It wasn't exactly a date. I'd been invited for dinner at her house, and it had just seemed kind of natural to suggest catching a movie at the mall afterward. I already liked Patsy, but I liked her even more when she told me she was into martial arts movies.

I was a bit worried that it'd be hard to make conversation, but so far we had lots to talk about. Clay told me that on his first date with my mom, he'd actually written up a list of stuff they could discuss. But in the end, he'd said, he hadn't had to use it.

"So what did you think of my mom's lasagna?" Patsy asked as we got closer to the ticket booth.

"She makes great meat sauce."

Patsy laughed. "You mean tofu sauce."

I gulped. "That was tofu? I hate tofu."

"I thought I hated it too. At first. Then I got used to it."

"Your mom and dad seem to be doing okay," I said. Patsy and I hadn't talked much about what had happened that day at her house, but I had this feeling I had to say something. After all, I knew more about her family than most people did. And of course, she knew a lot about me too.

"Mom's a lot happier now that Dad's in counseling for his gambling problem," Patsy said as casually as if we were still talking about lasagna. I looked around to check no one else was listening in. "Mom and I are gonna have to go too. For family counseling," Patsy added.

"They want me to go too," I said, dropping my voice.

When Patsy smiled, the skin around her eyes crinkled. "Family counseling is in," she said.

"It is?"

I was glad she let me pay for the tickets. "Do you want butter on your popcorn?" I asked her as we headed for the concession counter. There was a line there too. Oh well, I thought, that gives us more time to talk.

Patsy was the one who came up with the next topic. "Are you going to the trial?" she asked.

She was talking about the home invader, of course. Now that he was out of the hospital, he was going to be tried on nine counts of break and entry. I'd told Mom I wanted to go—even if it meant missing a few days of basketball camp. I'd talked Mom and Clay into enrolling me for another month.

"I'd like to go," I told her. Then I told Patsy something I hadn't told anybody else. "You know, I'm kind of relieved all the home invader had was a concussion. The thing is, I feel kind of connected to him. Like I understand him."

Patsy raised her eyebrows.

"Not the tying people up part, or stealing their stuff, or scaring them," I added quickly. "More the observing people part."

I felt Patsy's eyes scan my face as if she were looking for something. "Why can't you just observe them outside their houses? Like here, for instance." She lifted her eyes up toward the girl who was selling popcorn. The girl tugged at her hair net, then reached down to massage her lower back. You could tell she was eager to finish her shift.

"I can. I do. It's just that observing people is more interesting when they don't know you're watching them. Then you really get to know them."

This time Patsy nodded. I had the feeling she was starting to get it. "I guess it's like watching a movie—or reading a book," she said.

"Uh-huh," I told her.

Someone tapped my shoulder. It was my mom. She was with Clay. "What are you kids doing here?" my mom asked.

"Patsy and I figured we'd catch a movie after supper. We're going to see *Tae Foo Rumble*. What about you guys?"

Don't say you're going to see *Tae Foo Rumble*, I thought to myself.

No such luck.

"Us too," my mom said. "This is great. We can sit together. It'll be like a double date."

I felt my ears turn hot.

"Sure," Patsy said, in a voice that didn't sound so sure.

"You know, honey, now that I think about it, I'm not exactly in the mood for a martial arts movie," Clay said, taking my mom's elbow. "Wasn't there a chick flick you wanted to see? I'd bet they'd let us change our tickets."

My mom looked at him. "Sure," she said, "that sounds like a good idea. You two enjoy your movie, okay?"

"I thought you hated chick flicks," I heard

her tell Clay as they walked back to the ticket booth.

"A guy can get used to anything," he told her as he put his arm through hers. Even from behind, I could see his cowlick sticking up in the air.

Patsy had been watching them too. "So are you getting used to him?" she asked me.

I shrugged my shoulders. "I guess so," I said. "Just do me one favor, Patsy."

"Sure."

"Don't tell him."

OTHER TITLES IN THE ORCA SOUNDINGS SERIES

Also by Monique Polak

No More Pranks

Aunt Daisy's words rang in my head, like a song you can't forget, no matter how hard you try. "Three minutes until you lose sensation in your extremities."

I wriggled my fingers and toes. While I still could.

Pete likes to play pranks. It doesn't matter what it is as long as it gets a laugh. When he impersonates his vice-principal on a radio call-in show, he goes too far and is suspended from school. Pete's parents send him to spend the summer working with his uncle, a whale-watching guide in a tourist town far from the city. When a whale is injured by a reckless tour guide, Pete struggles to save the animal. Then Pete has to pull the most important prank of his life to bring the guide to justice.